AF506432

Copyright © 2024 by Author Name

Published by: Stellar Book Publishing
www.stellarbookpublishing.com

Christmas in June
Written By:
Sheilla Ignacio-deVega

Maria came from a poor family and an impoverished village. She had nothing but a Dream. She's thinking about how to get out of poverty and help her family in the future.

For her studying hard is the key to fighting back poverty. She received scholarships in high school and college to further hone her talent and intelligence.

She was always academically competitive, studied well, and was awarded in many quiz bees to sharpen her craft.

D.O.S.T.

During the days she was in college, she was advised to report her Semester grades to the Government and submit her grades to maintain the Scholarship.

One fine day the Semester ended, and she submitted her grades. Then her mentor mentioned, "You are really good!" But you know you need to balance and enjoy yourself and the life you have in college. Serve the community, your school, and your student body. Go out, meet others, and know

"How to make a difference."

Maria tried to make a difference. She joined the Student Organization in her school. She enjoyed meeting people and doing charitable work and outreach programs in school. She discovered she enjoyed serving people. To give back all the benefits she has been receiving from the Scholarship, she served the school and her fellow students, all her heart through the Organization.

Introducing Pepe.

Pepe is a picture of a Happy Family. They lived in a mountainside and everything is so perfect. They usually hang out in the mountain enjoying the beautiful flowers, the chirping of the birds, and the serenity of the surroundings. Everything is perfect, except for the daily struggle of living. His parents are working hard every day to supplement their needs in everyday living.

Pepe is a good kid and very mature to think of his age.
He always took care of his siblings, bathed, and fed them while
his dad and his mom were away working in the Mountain.
They were gathering wood to make coal and sell it. Planting
vegetables and selling them at the Market.

Pepe and his younger brother and sister needed to cross the
river to attend school.They were struggling in life.
They were living in a mountainside.

One night, he saw his mom and dad in

distress and were fighting.

Their mom left them and vanished

without a trace. His dad got

so quiet, sad, and depressed.

One day, after school he went home with his siblings.
They waited for their father to come back,
and it was dark. They didn't have
electricity and just used
wood and candles. No food on the table and
their stomach were trembling.
He saw plenty of potatoes and
cooked them for his younger siblings.

The night passed and he woke up at sunrise without his father arriving. And they were abandoned too by their father.

Crying for help he runs so fast and the rain starts pouring. A hunter found him. He brought him and his siblings to the Social Worker. And they were brought to Hospicio de San Lazaro in Manila.

Christmas is coming!
You gonna hear Christmas carols everywhere. People are singing everywhere! Everyone is in high spirits. People are all Smiles! Everyone is so cheerful, gift-giving is everywhere, and Christmas parties are. Christmas lights are blinking with different colors! Christmas lanterns are up everywhere to bring joy and a vibrant atmosphere!
merry Christmas
Nanay Dita's Sari-Sari Store
Bawal Utang Dito Lista Pwede!
Price
KARAOKE

So Maria thought it would be better to set up an outreach
program for the kids this December to
share that feeling of Festivities and offer some gifts
to the kids in Orphanage. So, she gathered the
meeting in the Organization and started setting up a
visit. She asked permission to have some of the kids
inside Hospicio de San Lazaro with representatives
from them. The plan is to tour
around the kids in the city and at the mall and
give them gifts.

Maria and her team arrived
at Hospicio de San Lazaro.
Everyone is so welcome
and happy. She and her
team granted permission
to tour around the kids with
representatives from the
Hospice. Two individuals
were assigned with one kid.
Maria and the other
representative from
Hospicio were assigned
to Pepe.

The bus is on the way to the mall. The city is in vibrant spirit.
The kids are excited. Singing, laughing, giggling with each other.
With signs of excitement and fun!

The mall is packed and in grander exhibits and decorations.
Christmas is one of the most festive seasons
to celebrate in a year.
Family is rushing to buy new clothes and new
pairs of shoes for their
kids, family, friends, and godsons and daughters.

All the kids were so happy and enjoying the mall except
for Pepe. He seemed so aloof and observed everyone.

At the Bus going Back to Hospicio:

Maria: Hi Pepe, are you alright?
Pepe: Yes I am. I am just overwhelmed. I just
thought about···hmm··some things, my other
siblings, and my Father·My younger siblings
have been adopted here since we came 5 years ago.
I have 2 siblings, 1 boy and 1 girl. Since they were
younger than me, I told them to adopt
them first so they'll have a good family for them
to take care of.
Maria: Oh I see. How long have you been here?
Pepe: It's in my 5th year. Very brief answer.
Silence in the bus···
Maria: Don't worry Pepe you will be alright.
Pepe: Thank you. Just a very brief response.
Pepe seemed aloof and quiet all the
time, unlike the other kids. He seemed
mesmerizing the place and enjoying it
but he didn't want to show it.

The bus arrived and dropped
them off at the Hospicio.

And Pepe ran and the rain began pouring.

Maria went after him ....

Maria: Thank you Pepe for trusting and

spending time with us.

Pepe: Thank you too for the

gifts and time.

Another silence
and deep thoughts
from Pepe.
Pepe: Maria,
can I ask you
something?
Maria: Yes sure,
what is it?

Pepe: Why are
you only going
here during the
Christmas season?

Pepe: Don't get me wrong, I am so happy. I am so happy today and every DECEMBER. People visit us almost every week and give gifts. But after this, I will wait and wait, months and months, with fewer and fewer visitors every month until the Christmas season again to experience this. After this, I am gonna be sad again and count how many more days to come before Christmas.

Pepe is sobbing with head down. Tears run down his face.

Maria was left deft-mouthed and had some deep thoughts to respond.

Pepe: Can we make Christmas in June too?

Maria: Pepe think of it as a temporary thing,
someday you will have a Family that can give
you Christmas every day!
Just pray and pray and you will be alright.
These gifts are just ordinary instruments to
give you hope and temporary happiness.
The bottom line is that
the Christmas spirit
should be in your
heart no matter
what the days
are to give you
Hope to move
on with your past
life and make you
Smile. Forgive
yourself and forgive
those people who
made you wrong.
And live life to
the fullest wherever
you are and
wherever you go.
Thank you for being
open with me.
God loves you!

They hugged each other
and Maria left with tears
too on her face.

Ten years later, Pepe already graduated from College and became a successful Engineer. He has been adopted by a wealthy and caring Family. He finally got in touch with his two other siblings. He later found out that his father didn't leave them, but was found roaming around the nearby city, walking, crying, and talking to himself. He lost himself. He suffered from depression and mental illness. And was treated in the Mental Hospital for some years. Every year, he visits Hospicio de San Lazaro to give some of his earnings to charity and spend time with kids.

Maria has her own Family and became a successful Architect and at the same time a Social Worker and devoted her free time to Charitable Institutions. She got all the recognition during her Student days, but what touched her and opened a new perspective in her life, was when she met "Pepe." And she finally understood her Mentor and Counselor on how to make a difference in other's lives.

Maria and Pepe still keep in touch with
each other. And Maria felt she somehow
made a difference in one life!

DEDICATION

I dedicate this book to my husband, Rocky
who have influenced, loved, and guided me in many ways.

To my kids, Bao, Eddard, and Rocky Laurence who give me
the reason to wake up each day no matter
how the world is.

To all my Family and Friends, who guided and
inspired me along the way.
Thank you so much.

To you, Dear Reader,
Thank you for giving your Time and Chance to read
this Book.

For every reader who finds a
piece of themselves within these
chapters.

For All your Pain, Loss and fears
lift them up to the Lord.
And you'll Find Hope, Love, and Live again.

I also Dedicate this book to All the
Mentors and Coaches, Teachers, Children,
Mental and Health, and Scholarships'
Institutions and Organizations
that are continuously
helping the needy children and people
in our Society.

www.ingramcontent.com/pod-product-compliance
Lightning Source LLC
Chambersburg PA
CBHW041153150726
48006CB00015B/1964